Adventures of a Far Away Bear

Look Out, London!

June Earle

A catalogue record for this book is available from the National Library of Australia

Copyright © 2018 June Earle

All rights reserved.

ISBN: 1 876922869

ISBN-13: 978-1-876922-38-2

2nd Edition

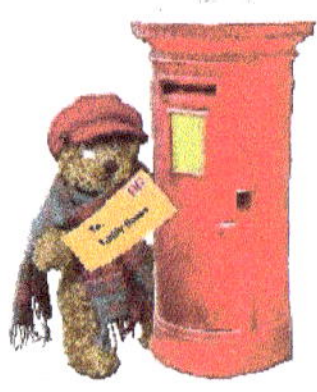

Teddy Books at Linellen Press
265 Boomerang Road
Oldbury, Western Australia, 6121

www.linellenpress.com.au

Dedication

For my daughter-in-law, Colette, who loves teddies as much as I do.

Adventures of a Far Away Bear

Acknowledgments

Thanks for the helpful cooperation from staff at London Underground and the London Eye Wheel.

Look Out, London!

"Liverpool Street Station, Dusty, is one of the busiest stations in London with over 63 million passengers coming and going each year."

"*Woof.* Is that more than a hundred? Why are people staring at us?"

"Probably haven't seen a bear wearing a tartan scarf before. Where we are standing now there were graves of people who died in the plague a long, long, long time ago."

"*Woof.* What's a plague?"

"A sickness that killed a lot of people."

"*Woof.* I don't think it is nice for a railway to be built on top of them."

"They removed all the skeletons and buried them in a special cemetery."

Information

Over 3,000 skeletons were removed from part of the Bedlam burial ground used for victims of the Civil War, The Great Plague of 1665 and the Great Fire of London 1666.

Liverpool Street Station is one of the four stations on the London version of the game Monopoly.

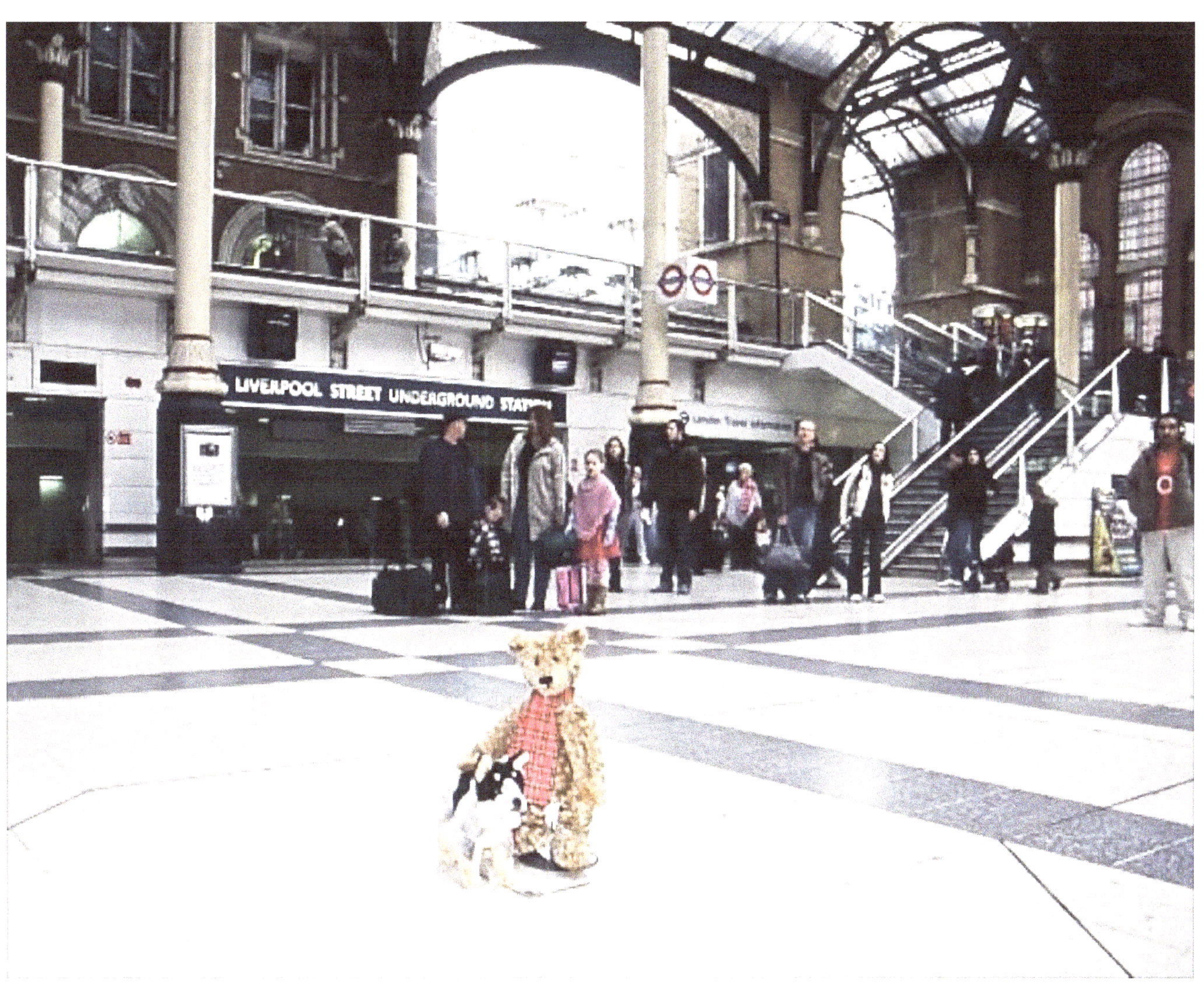

LIVERPOOL STREET UNDERGROUND STATION

"This is Trafalgar Square, built to commemorate the Battle of Trafalgar on the sea by Admiral Lord Nelson. The lions guard Horatio Nelson's Column and the Fountain. The lions are made out of the bronze melted from cannons taken in naval battles.

"Interesting, Dusty, that when they were digging here they found remains of a rhinoceros, elephant and hippopotamus."

"*Woof.* There sure is a lot of stuff under London. Can I dig a hole to find something?"

Information

Seventeen bus routes pass around Trafalgar Square. It is the biggest square in London and is owned by the Queen. Over 15 million tourists visit Trafalgar Square every year.

Fossilised bones of prehistoric animals were discovered here when digging the site.

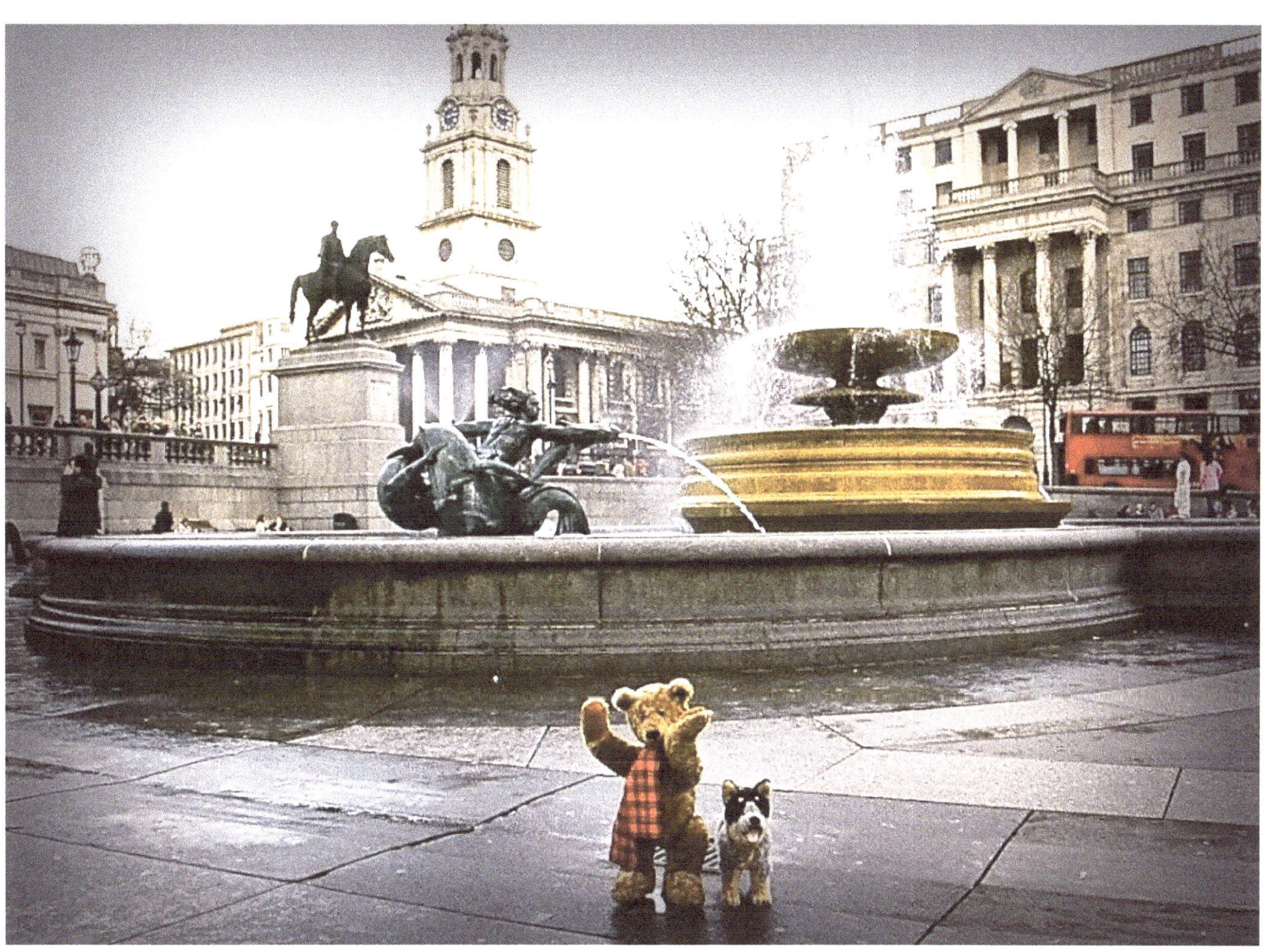

"*Woof.* I want to go and see the funny clock."

"We are not allowed through here. Big Ben is a bell and that is the tower it rings the time from. They call it the Great Clock of Westminster. It weighs over 13 tons or over 13 thousand kilograms. Listen, it is about to go Ding Dong."

"*Woof.* How did they get the big bell way up there?"

"It took 18 hours to pull it up by ropes and pulleys."

"*Woof.* I'm glad your clock is not that loud. We wouldn't be able to sleep."

Information

The clock face is cleaned with soap and water about every 5 years.

The Keeper of the clock and several clock engineers have to wind the clock three times a week to ensure the clock keeps the right time. It also has to be reset for Daylight Saving. Often the light bulbs that light Big Ben at night have to be changed.

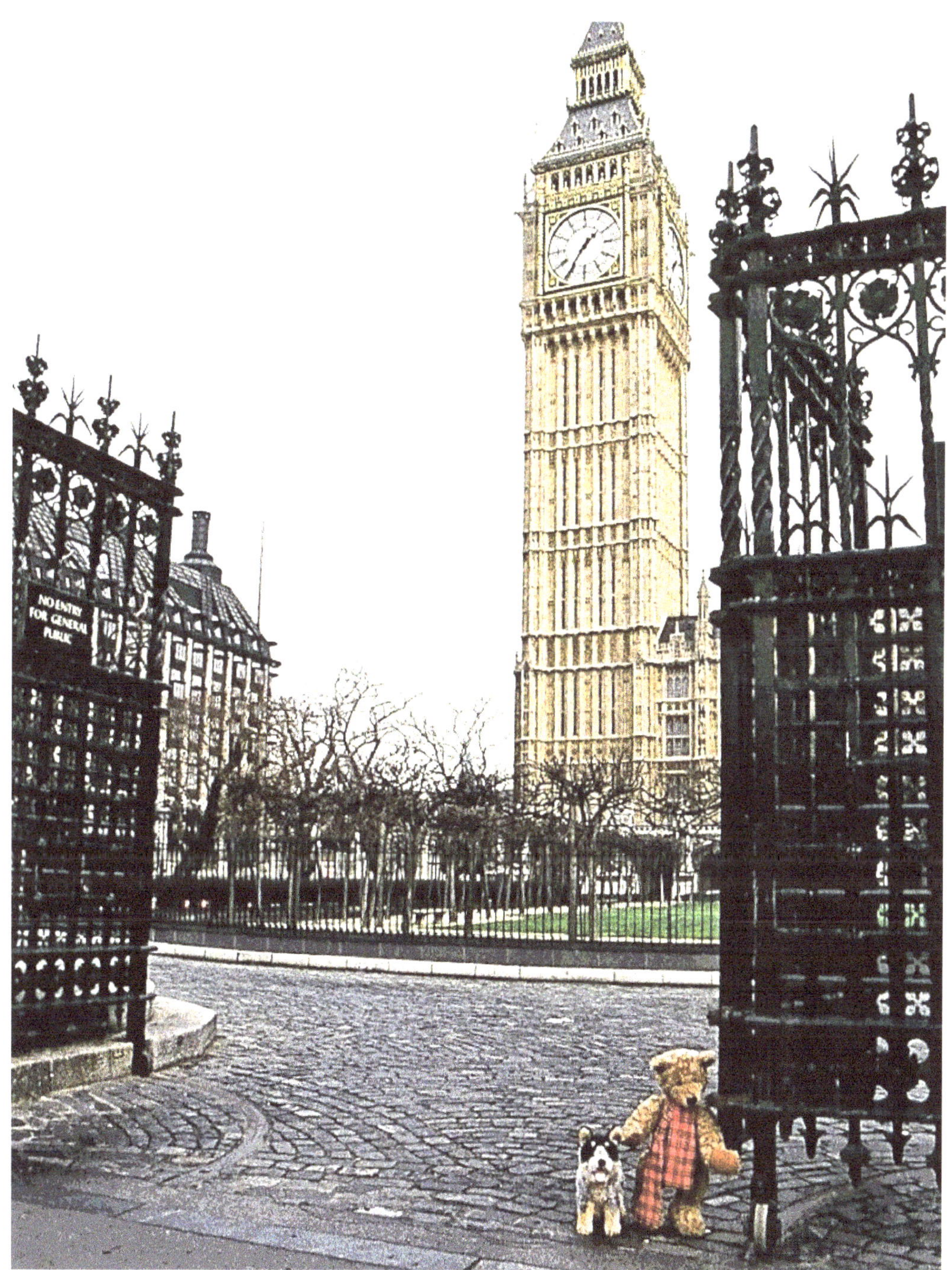
NO ENTRY
FOR GENERAL
PUBLIC

"*Woof*. Let's climb on the cannon."

"The Turkish Gun in Horse Guards Parade was captured by the British in a battle during the Napoleonic Wars in 1802."

"*Woof*. Napoleon … he's the man who wears that funny hat that looks like an upturned boat. Let's pull the cork out and see if it will go bang."

"No. It might frighten the Queen."

Information

Horse Guards Parade is a large open space used for special ceremonies.

So the gun would never fire again the British rammed the cork into the gun's mouth. After its capture at Alexandria during the Napoleonic wars it was placed in Horse Guards Parade in 1802.

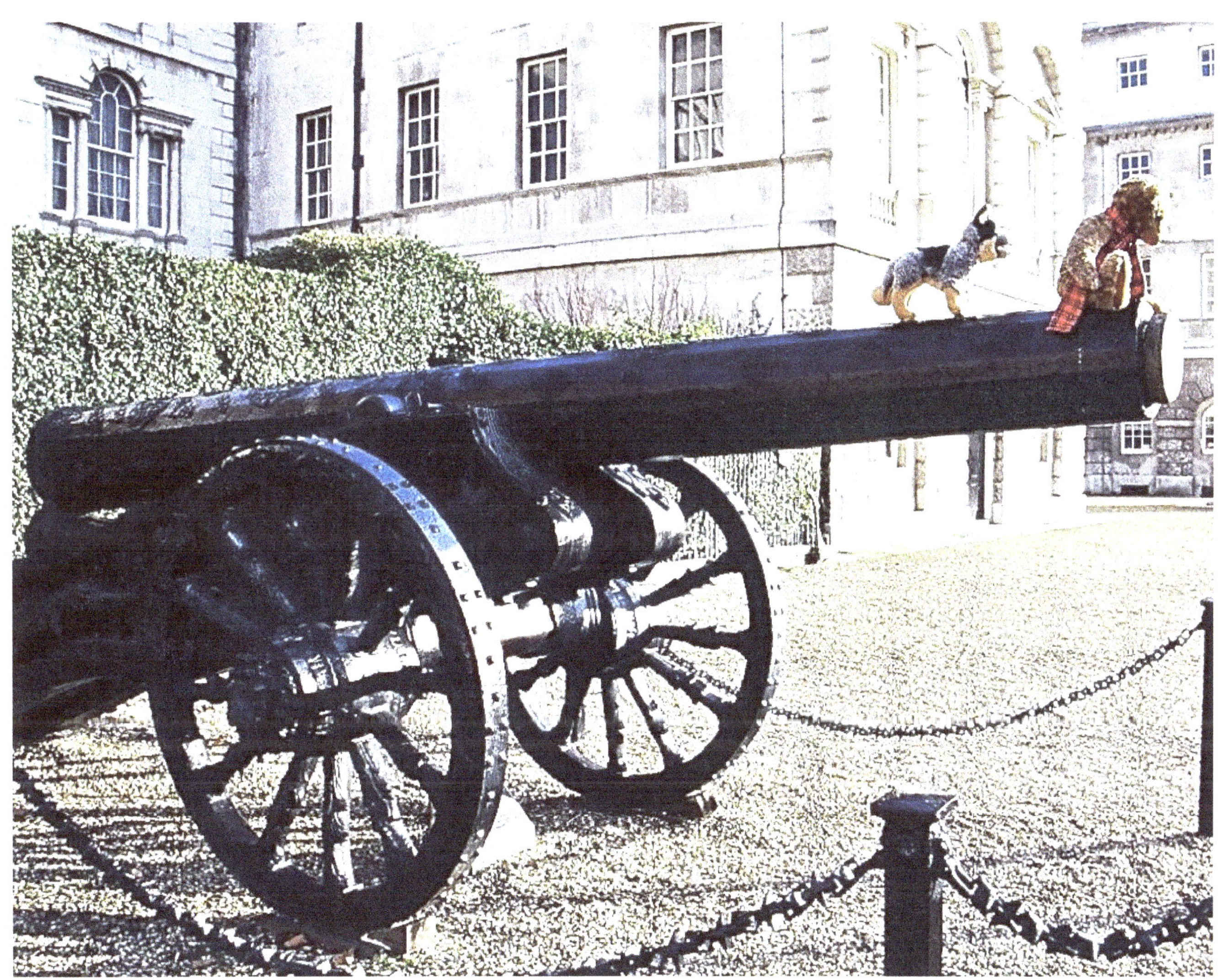

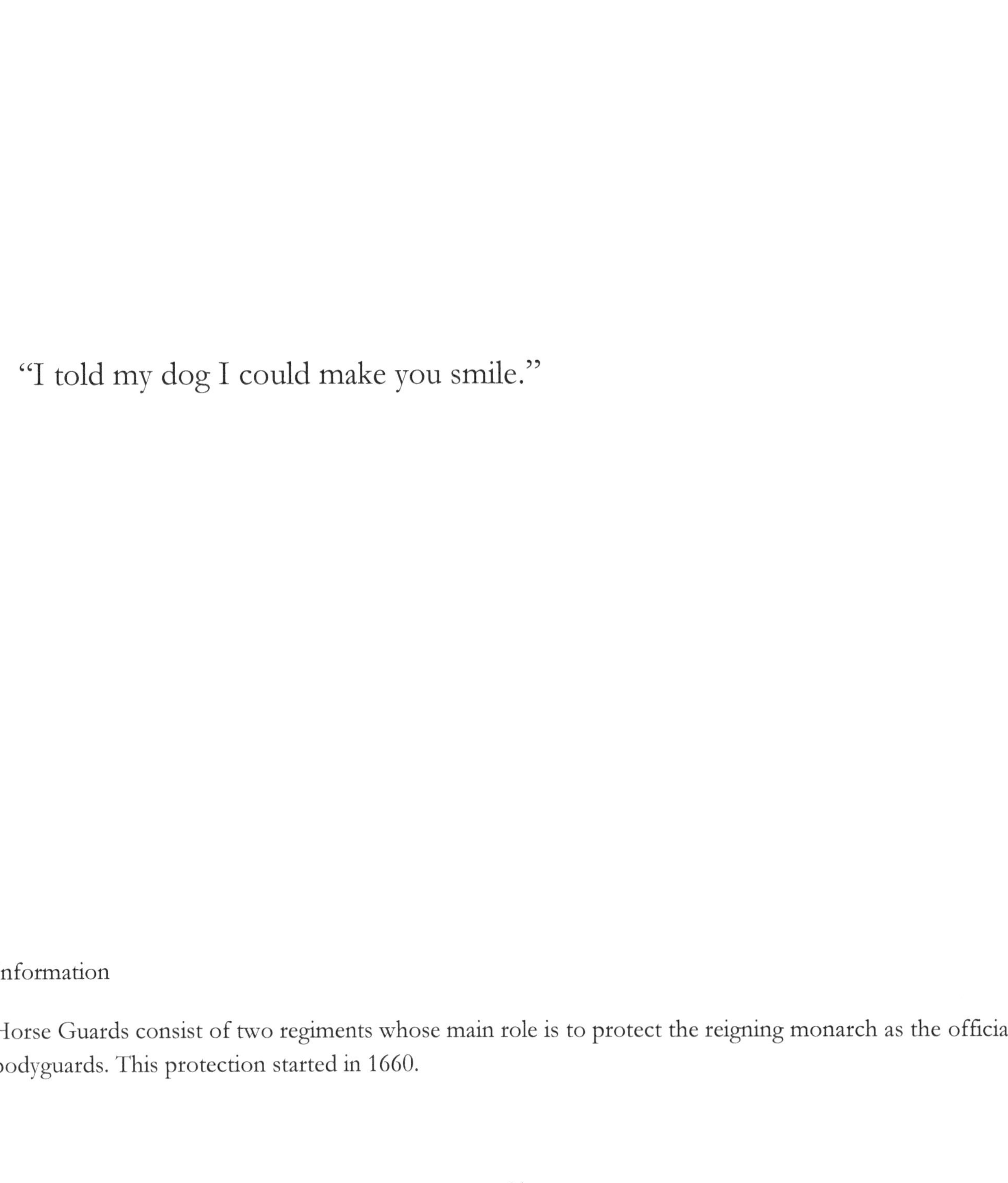

"I told my dog I could make you smile."

Information

Horse Guards consist of two regiments whose main role is to protect the reigning monarch as the official bodyguards. This protection started in 1660.

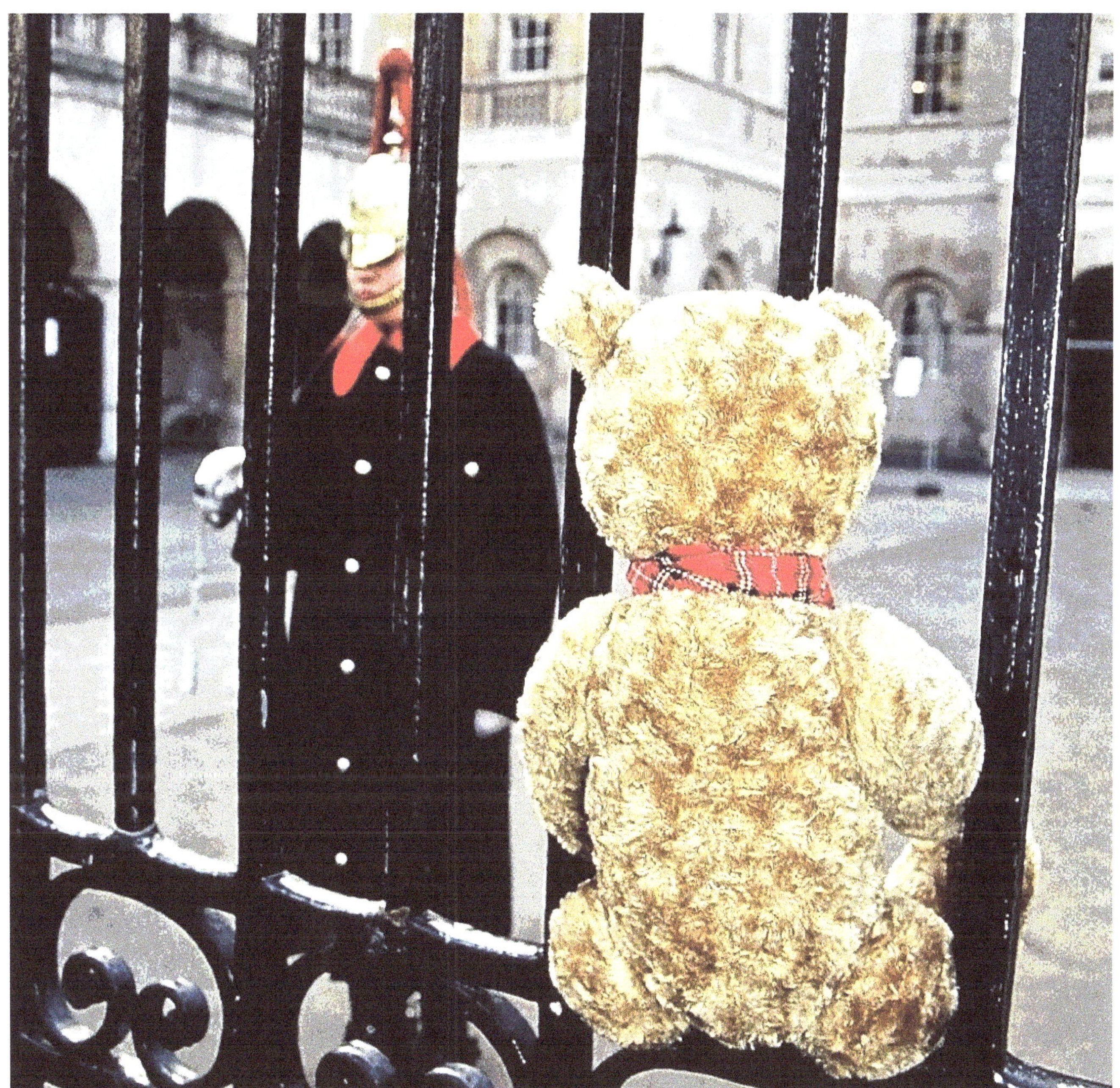

"Lady, I think the horse is asleep and this guard won't smile either. If you put me up on the horse I could tickle him."

Information

Black horses are used by most of the Horse Guard regiment and greys by Trumpeters. Over 90% of the horses come from Ireland. They have to be big and strong to carry the weight of a fully dressed officer and saddle.

Retirement age of the horses is between 17 or 18 years of age.

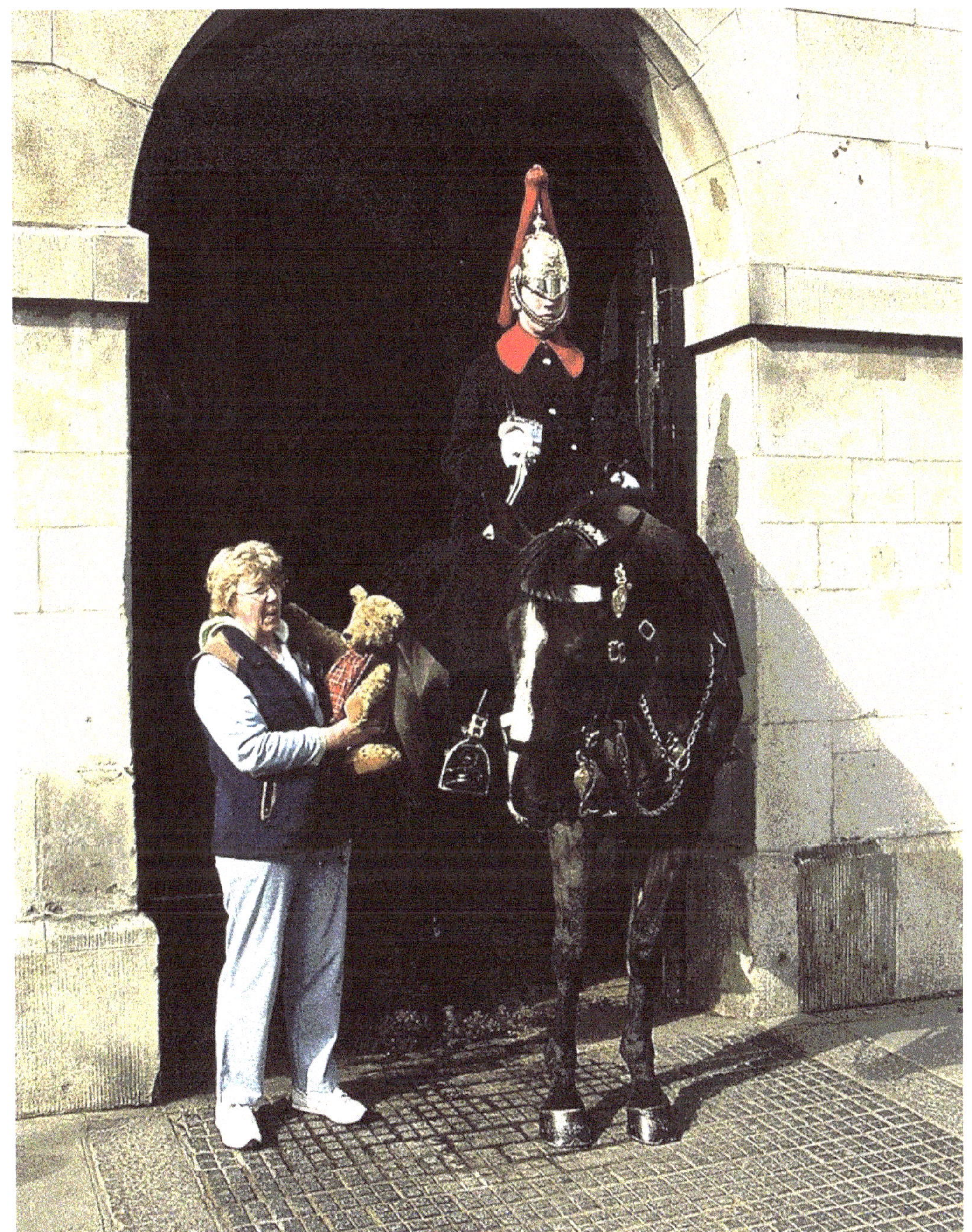

"*WOOF! WOOF! WOOF!*"

"Yes, YES! We will go and see Big Ben soon. I must try and find out where Uncle Willy is first."

"*Woof.* I think he'll be looking at Big Ben."

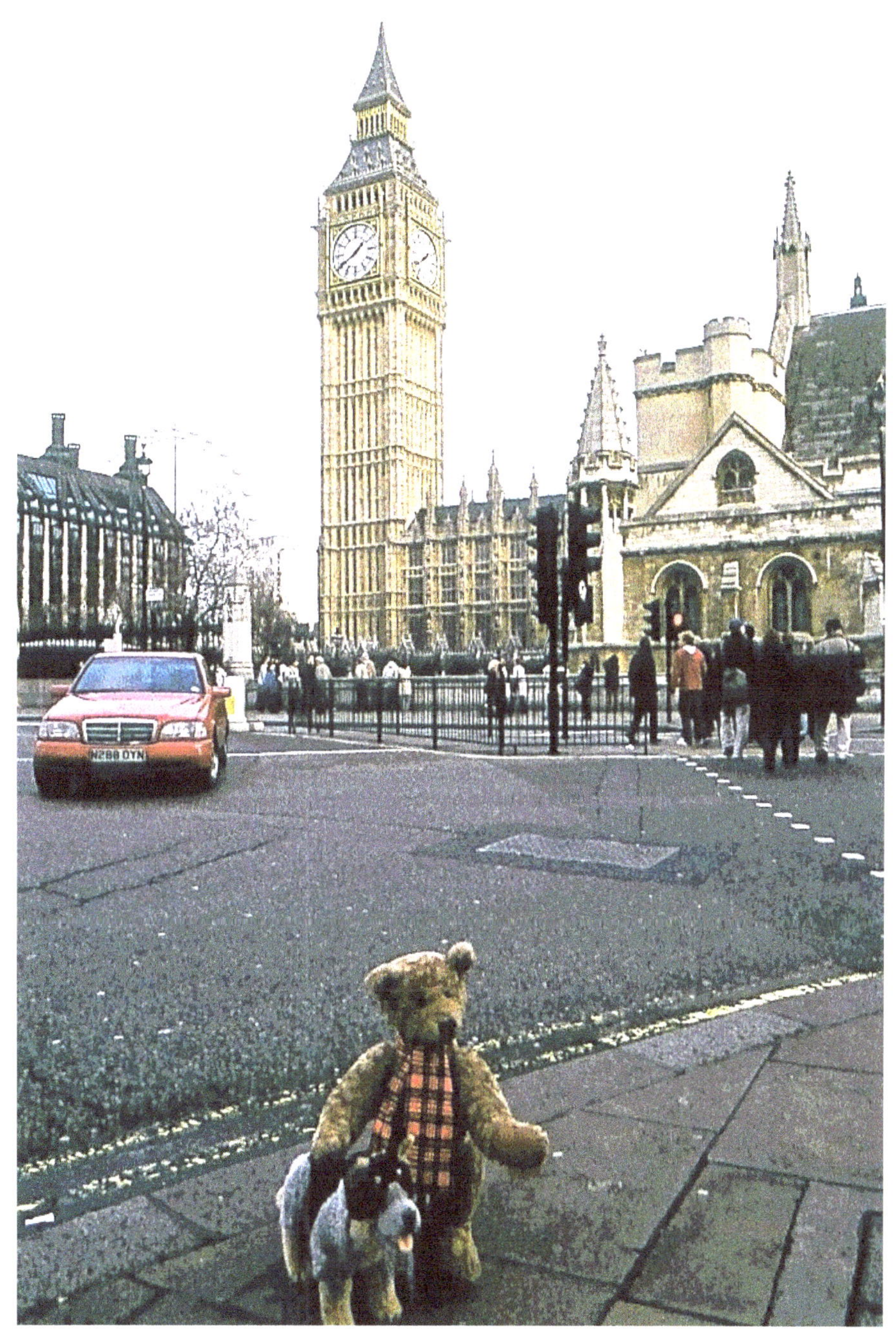

"*Woof.* All this history is making me hungry."

"Westminster Abbey plays a very important part in our history. Since 1066 it has been a place to go and say your prayers. Nearly every King and Queen has been crowned in there including our Queen Elizabeth the II.

"*Woof.* Do royal dogs get crowned?"

"No."

Information

The first coronations were Harold of Wessex and William the Conqueror.

The first wedding took place in 1100 between King Henry 1st and Matilda of Scotland.

An oak door by the Chapter House in the cloister behind the abbey has been carbon dated back to Edward the Confessor between 1032 AD and 1064AD.

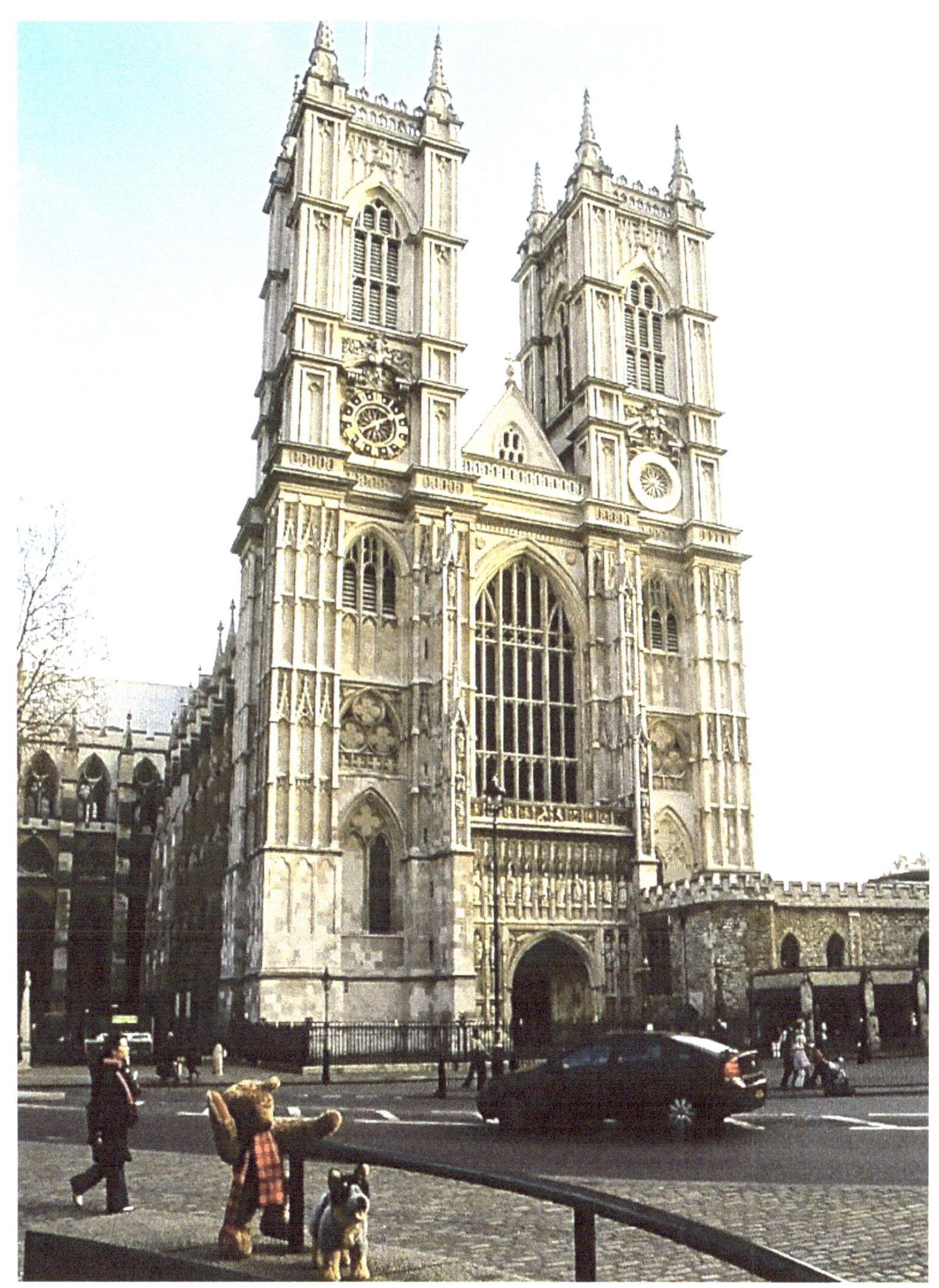

"*Woof.* What are those red things?"

"Old style telephone booths. Let's see if we can phone Uncle Willy."

"*Woof.* They would make great two storey kennels."

"The lady at the hotel said he has gone to Ireland to find Leprechauns."

"*Woof.* What are Leprechauns?"

"Little men who wear green suits and get up to mischief."

"*Woof.* Just like me."

Information

The paint colour is called current red so the telephone booths can easily be seen. The first booth was made out of concrete in 1920. Green booths have now been introduced and are run on solar power and can be used to recharge mobile phones.

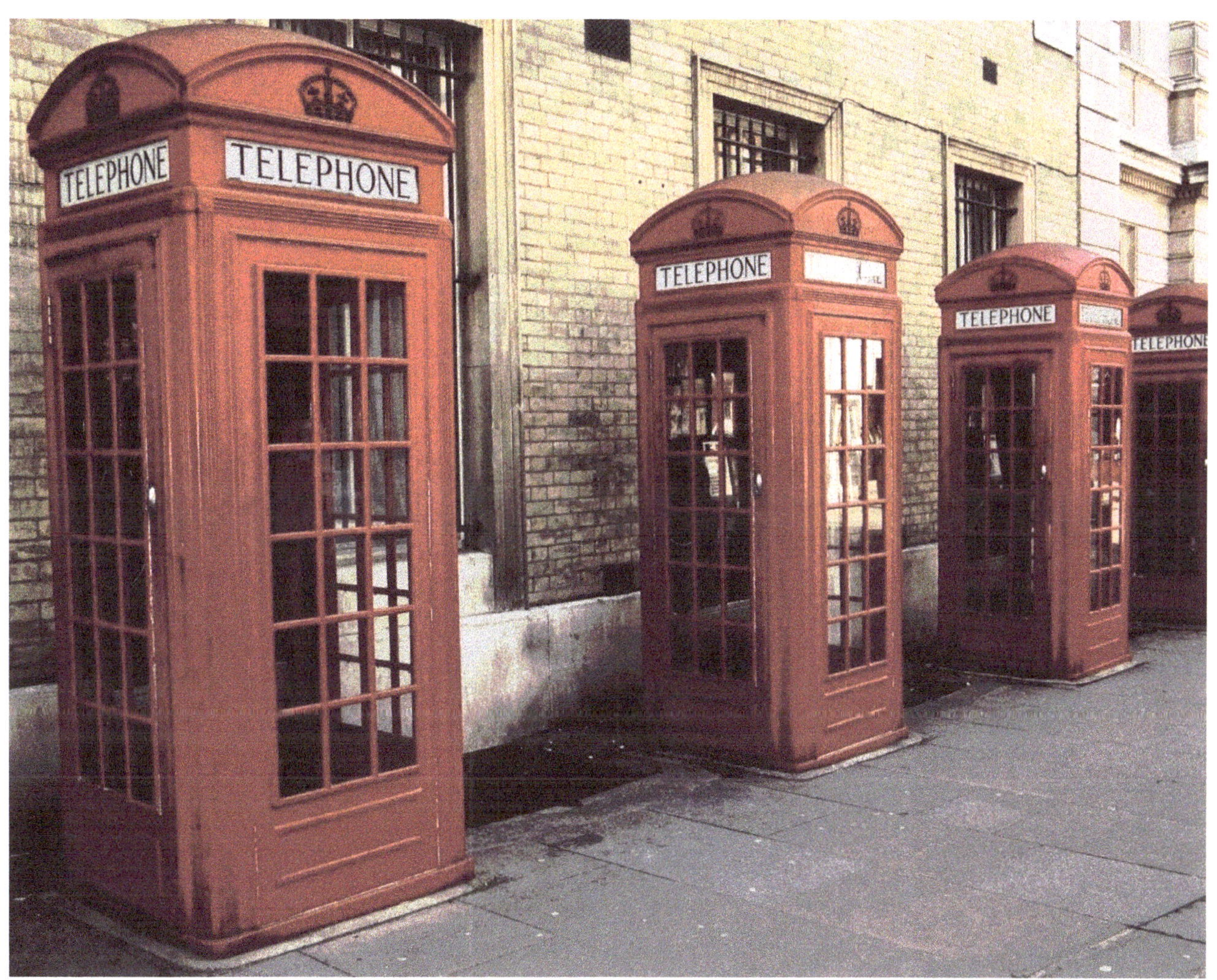

TELEPHONE
TELEPHONE
TELEPHONE
TELEPHONE
TELEPHONE
TELEPHONE

"I told you we couldn't take a shortcut to see Big Ben through here. NO ENTRY! Includes dogs."

"*Woof.* The big policeman got cross, didn't he? I really wasn't going to bite him."

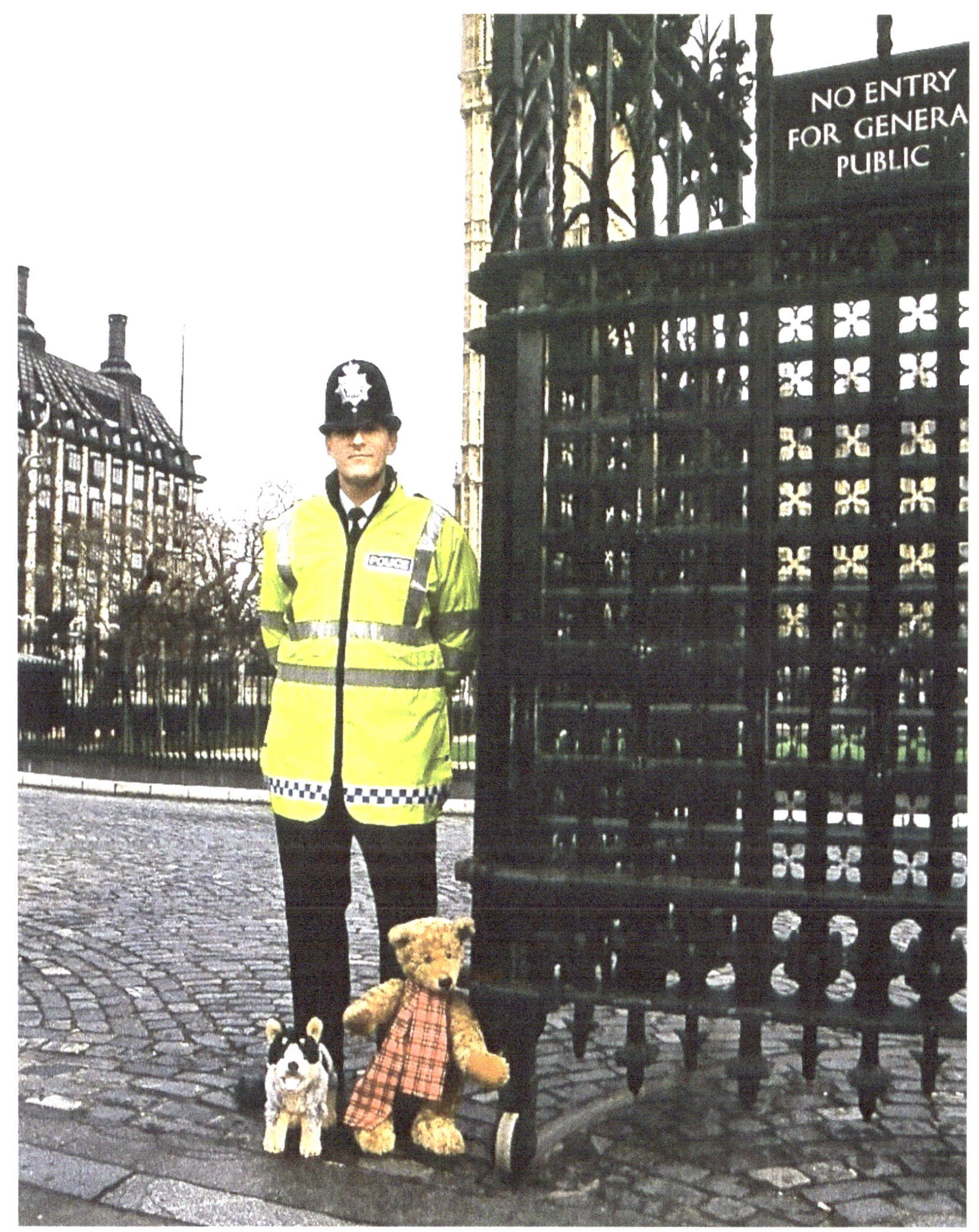

NO ENTRY
FOR GENERA
PUBLIC
POLICE

"*Woof.* Ask him if we can ride in his car – I like red."

"No, Dusty, you can't ask the policeman to give you a ride in the police car. This is a red car which means it is important."

"*Woof.* Okay, do they have other colours we can have a ride in? A yellow one would be good. I like yellow."

Information

Red cars are used by special operations: Diplomatic Protection and Law enforcement.

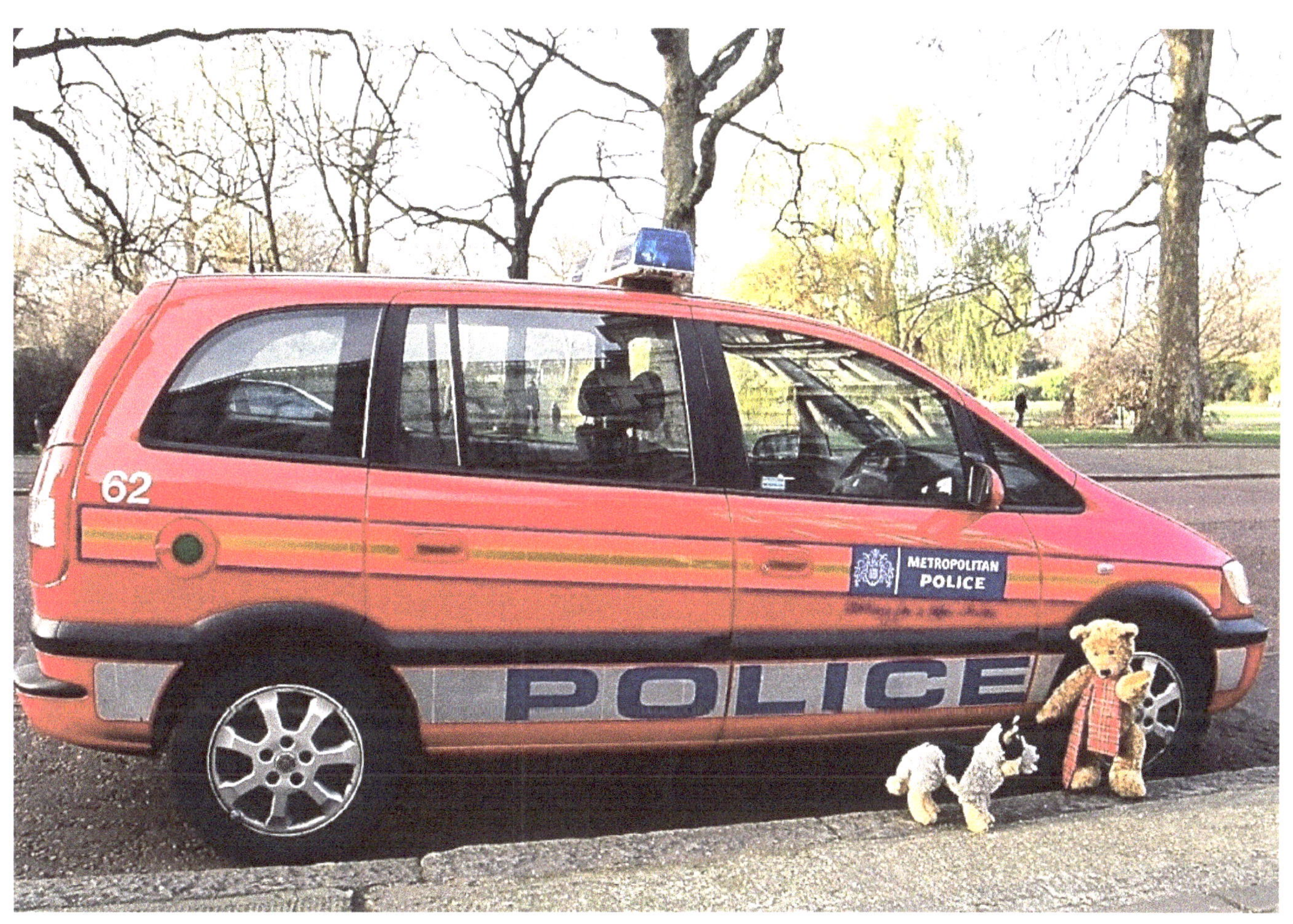
62
METROPOLITAN
POLICE
POLICE

"That is Tower Bridge. It took 8 years to build it across the River Thames. It opens up so tall ships can go through."

"*Woof.* Do the cars fall into the water?"

"No. Cars are stopped from crossing when it is opening. There is a weight limit too, no more than 18 tons."

"*Woof.* We're okay then."

Information

In 1952 a double-decker bus was crossing when the bridge began to open. The bus driver accelerated and jumped a three feet gap. He was awarded ten pounds for his bravery.

Ships always have right of way.

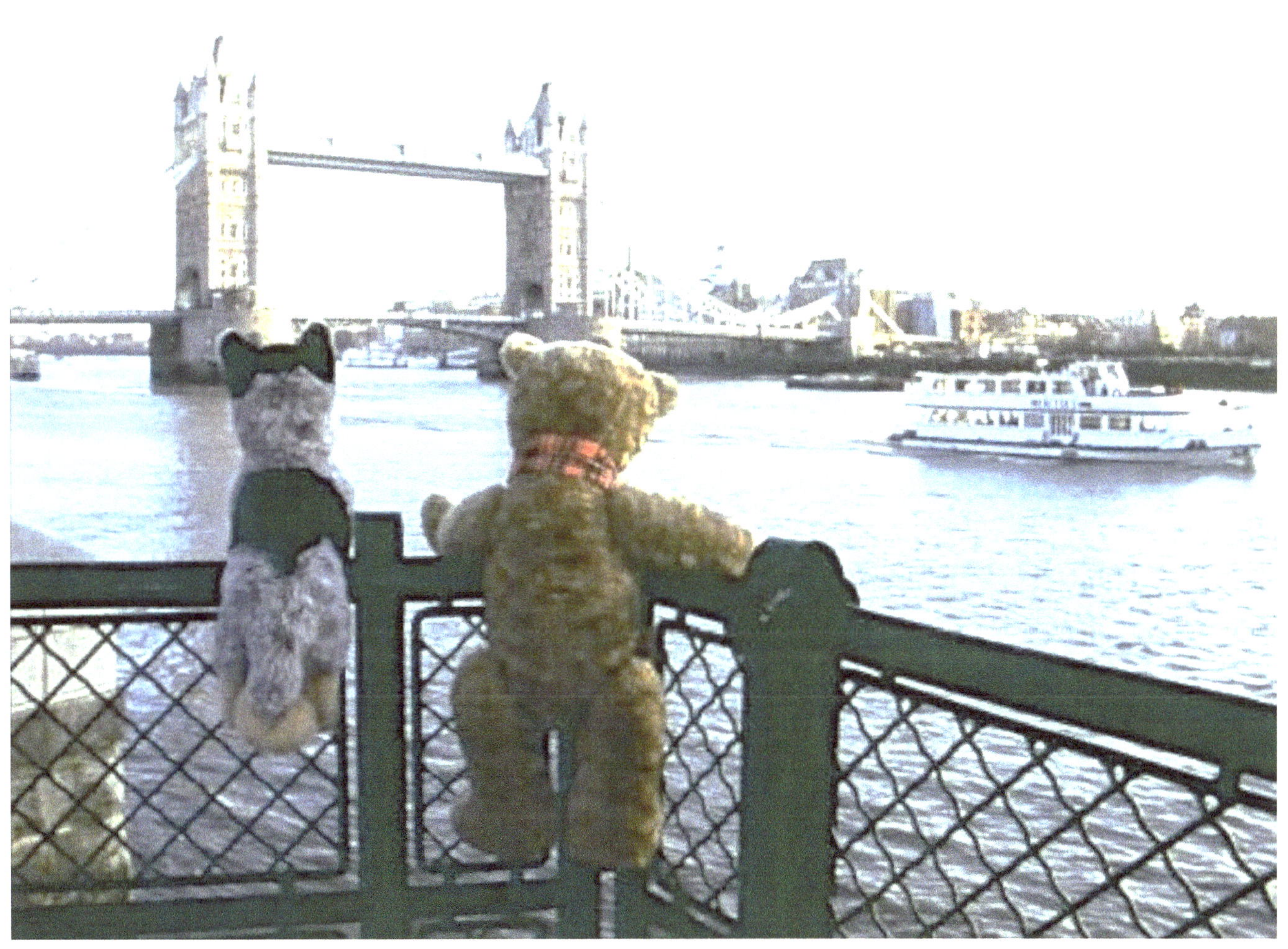

"Look, Dusty, let's take a tour on the big red double-decker bus."

"*Woof.* I want to ride up top."

"Good idea. We can travel all around London and see the sights from up there."

Information

The red double-decker buses are a national symbol of London. Before the upper deck had a roof on it you only had to pay half price to ride up top.

Many retired double-decker buses have been converted into mobile homes or cafes. Cliff Richards used one for his Summer Holiday movie.

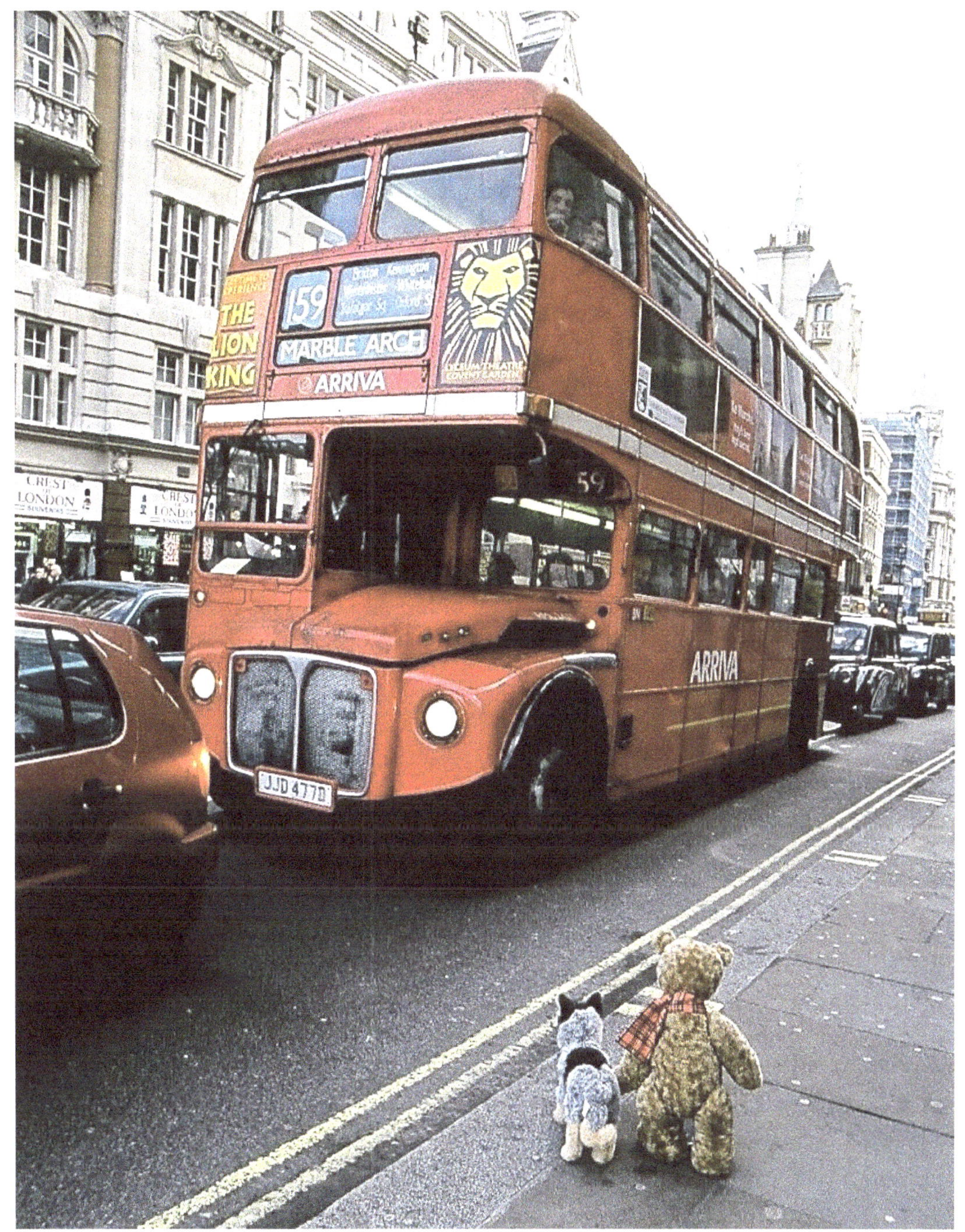

159
MARBLE ARCH
ARRIVA
THE LION KING
LYCEUM THEATRE
COVENT GARDEN
59
ARRIVA
JJD 477D

"That big circle thing is a Ferris wheel called the London Eye."

"*Woof.* What is it looking at? Why does it only have one eye?"

"We will go for a ride and find out."

"*Woof.* Do they have parachutes for dogs? I don't want to go spinning around."

"It is very slow, just like a tortoise. You won't feel it going round."

"*Woof.* Why is everything up over here?"

Information

When your capsule arrives at the top you are able to see up to forty kilometres away, on a good day. It takes about 30 minutes to do a full circle. It can carry up to 800 people on it per revolution. It is really a cantilevered observation wheel.

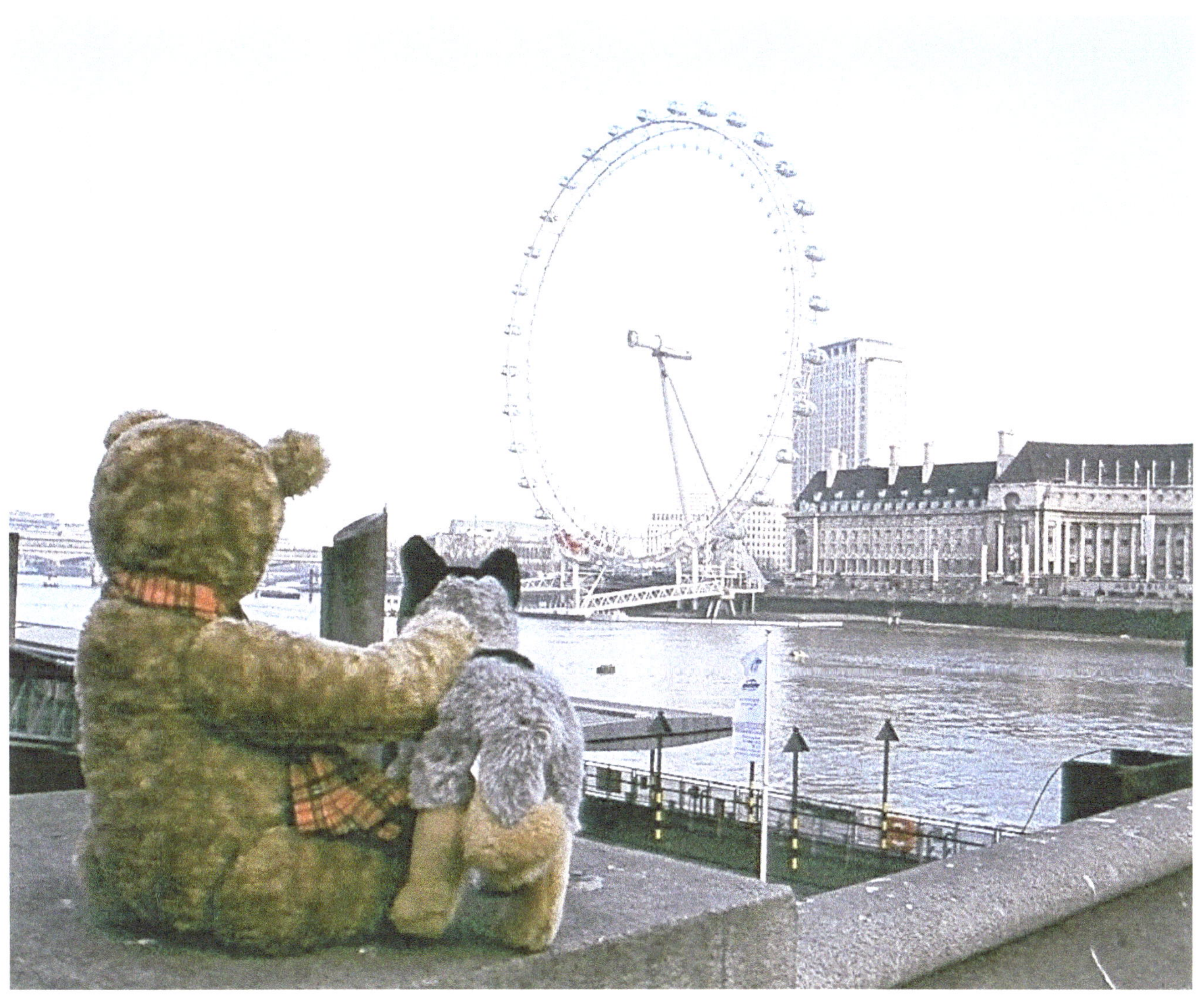

"Look, Dusty, there is a boat."

"*Woof.* When does this thing go down?"

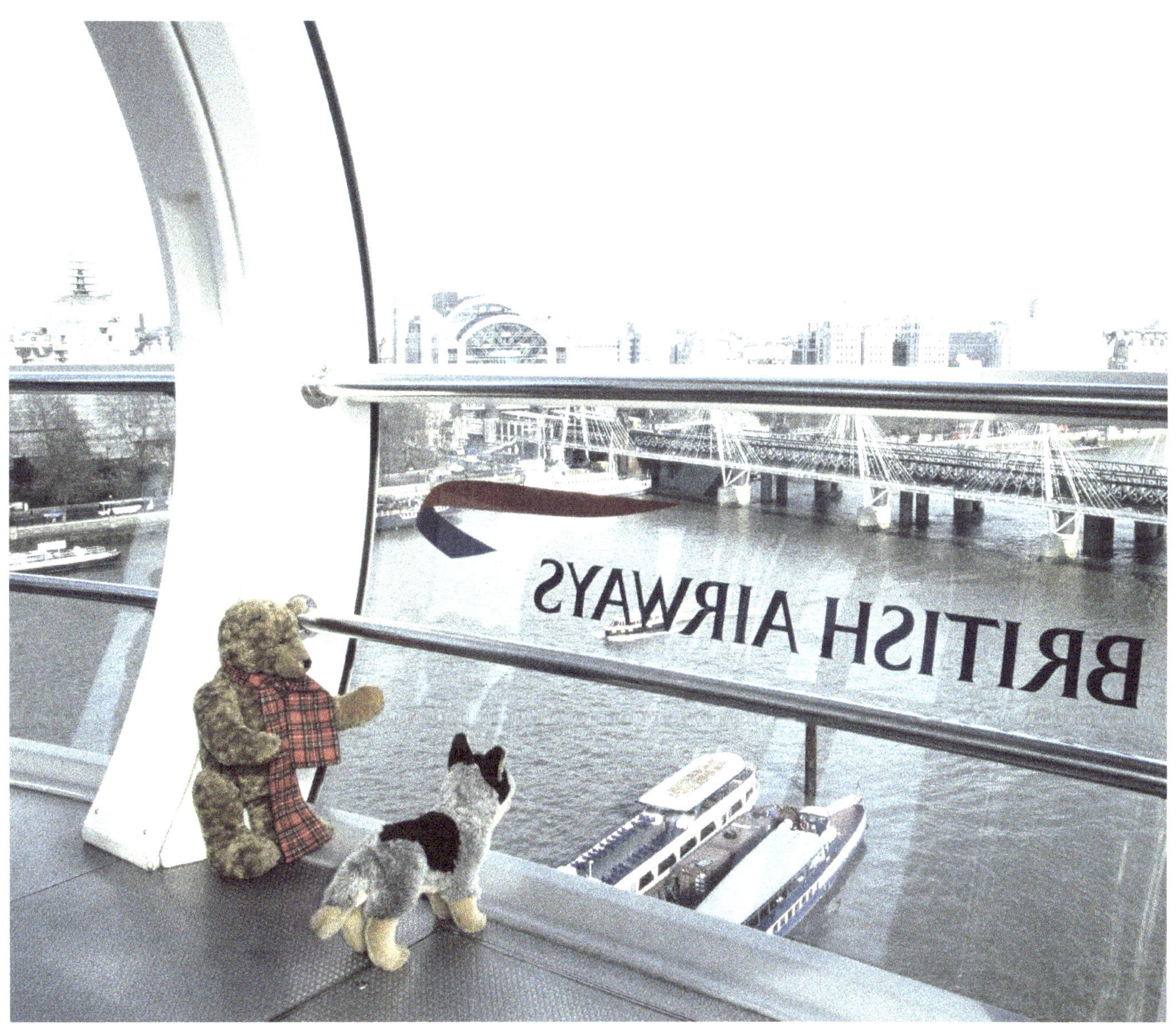

BRITISH AIRWAYS

"Look, Dusty, we can see a capsule on the big wheel."

"*Woof.* I think I'm wheelie, wheelie, sick. Are we there yet?"

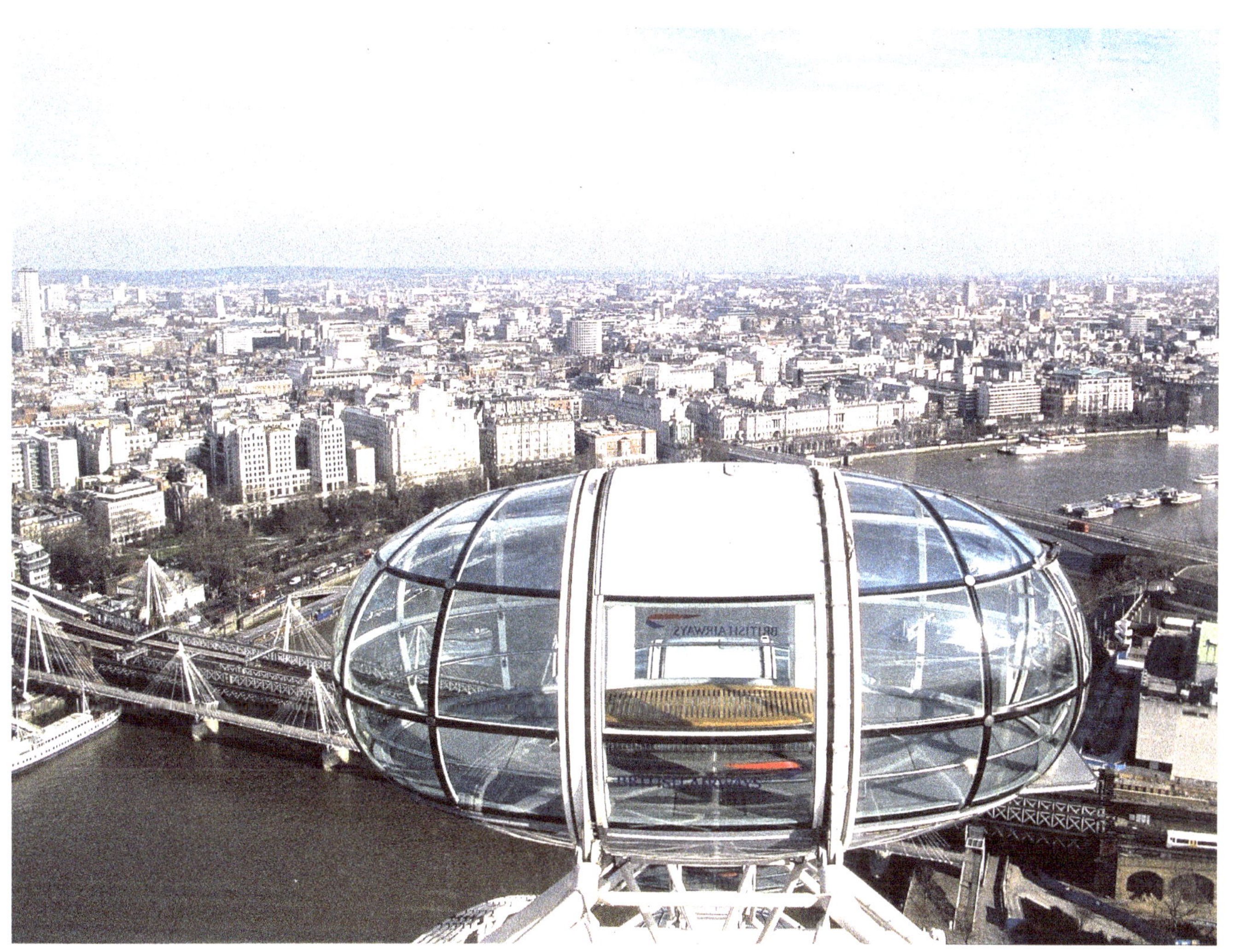

"Up, up, we go. Isn't this fun, Dusty? I wonder if Uncle Willy had a ride on this?"

"*Woof*. Fun is chasing my tail or digging a hole."

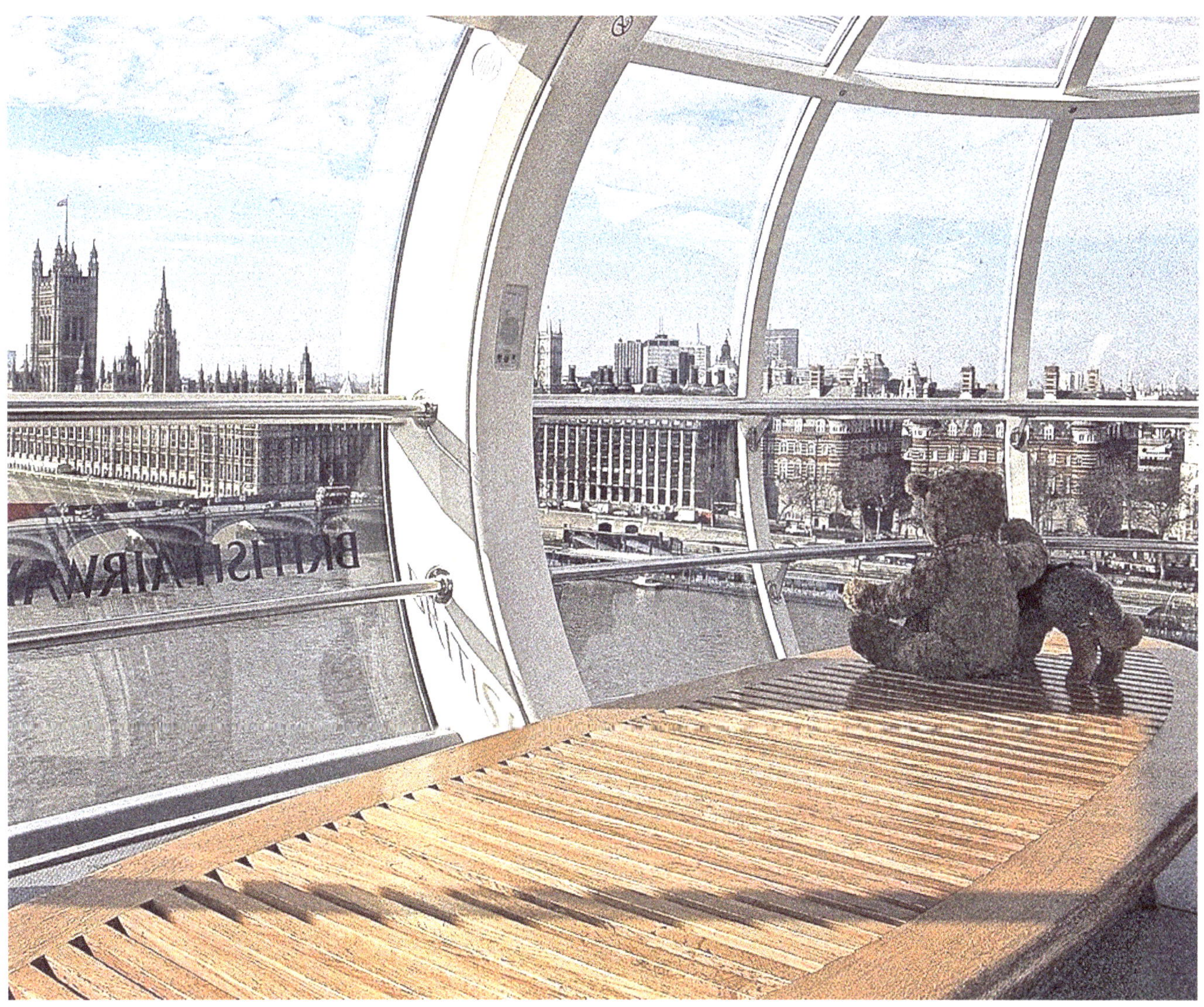

BRITISH AIRWAYS

"Dusty, you can see Big Ben."

"*Woof*. I'd rather be on the ground looking up at it."

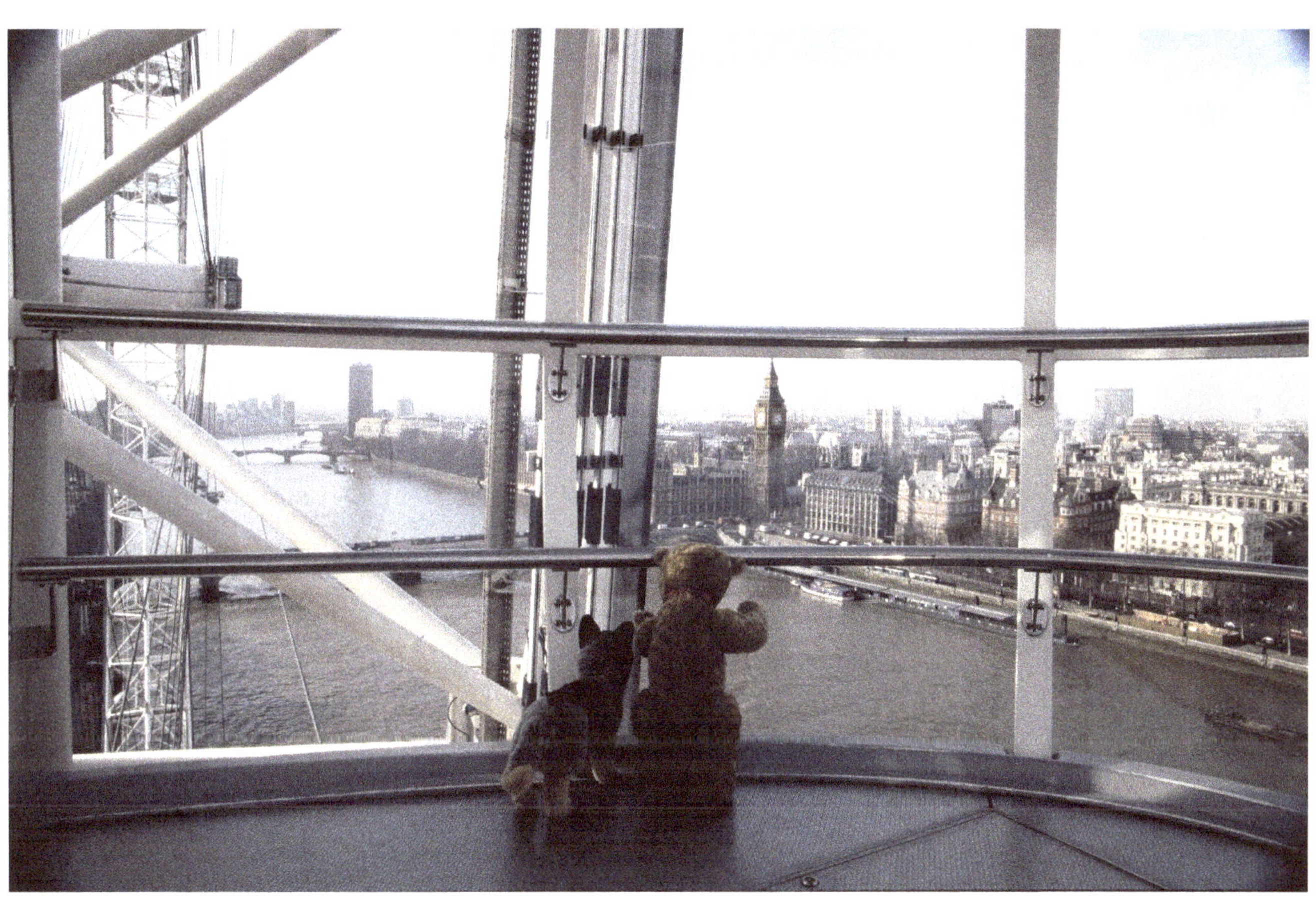

"I can see way up the River Thames from here."

"*Woof.* Are we at the top yet?"

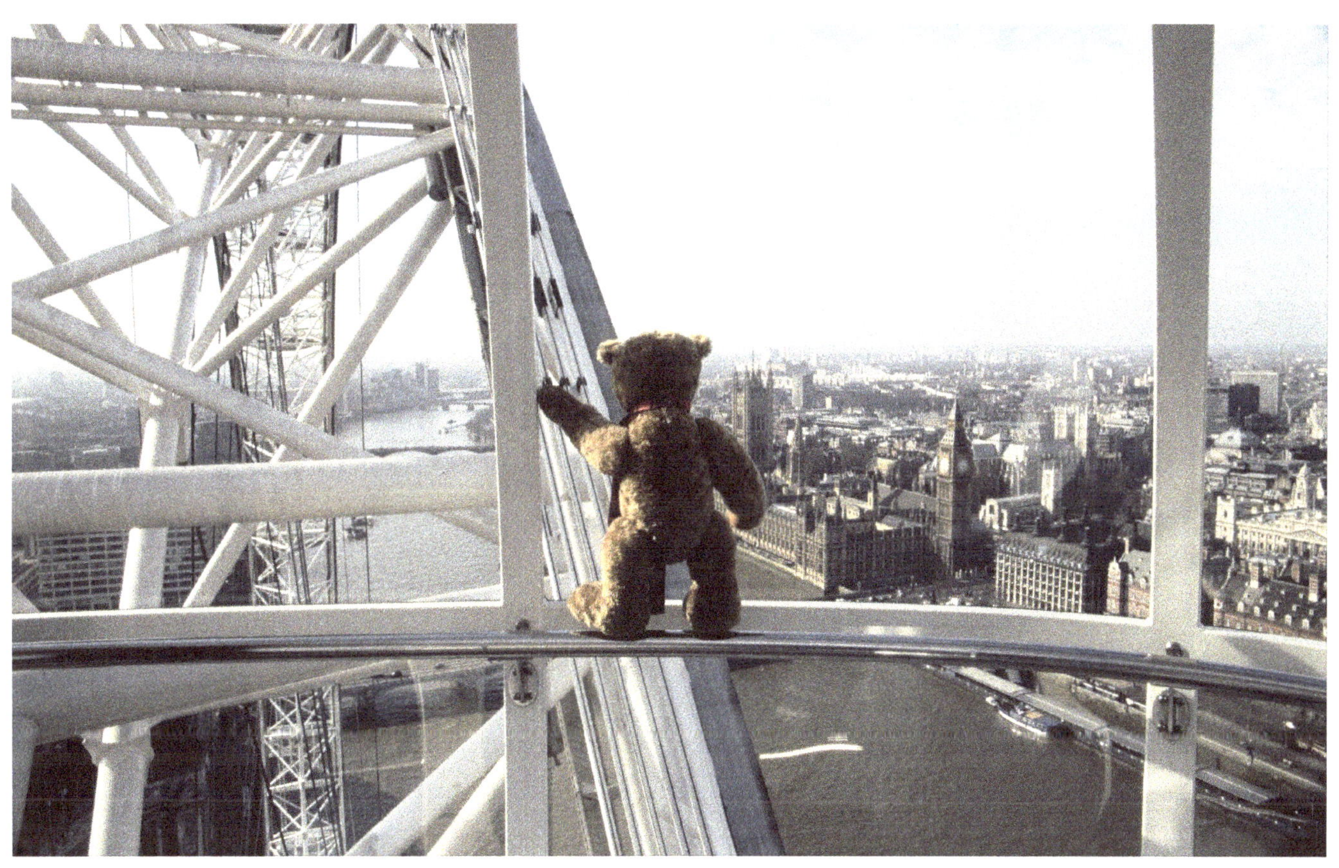

"DUSTY! Open your eyes."

"*Woof.* I will when we get down."

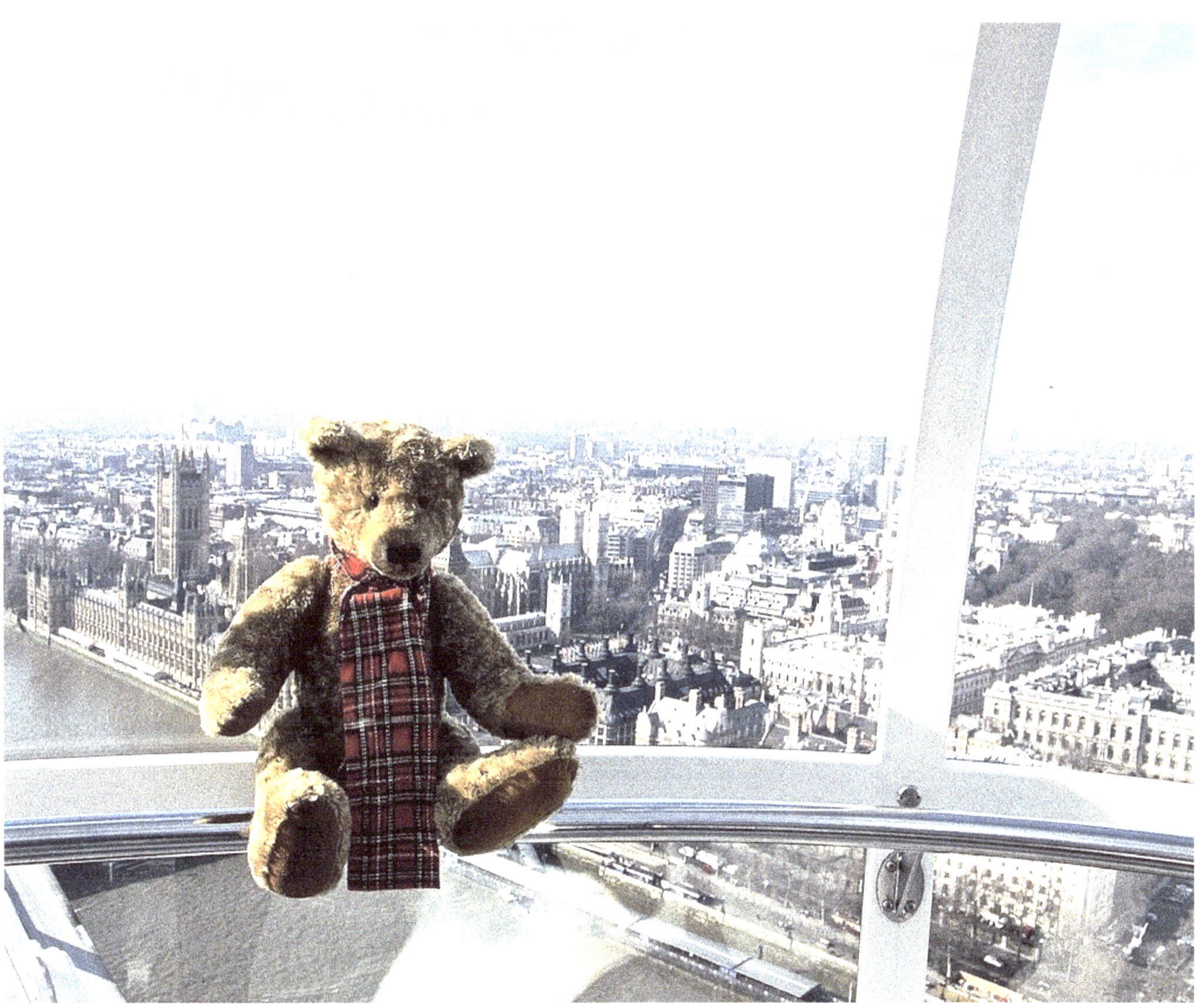

"No, we can't go back and say goodbye to Big Ben. Hurry up, Dusty, before everyone else gets on board the train. Next stop we pick up our home on wheels."

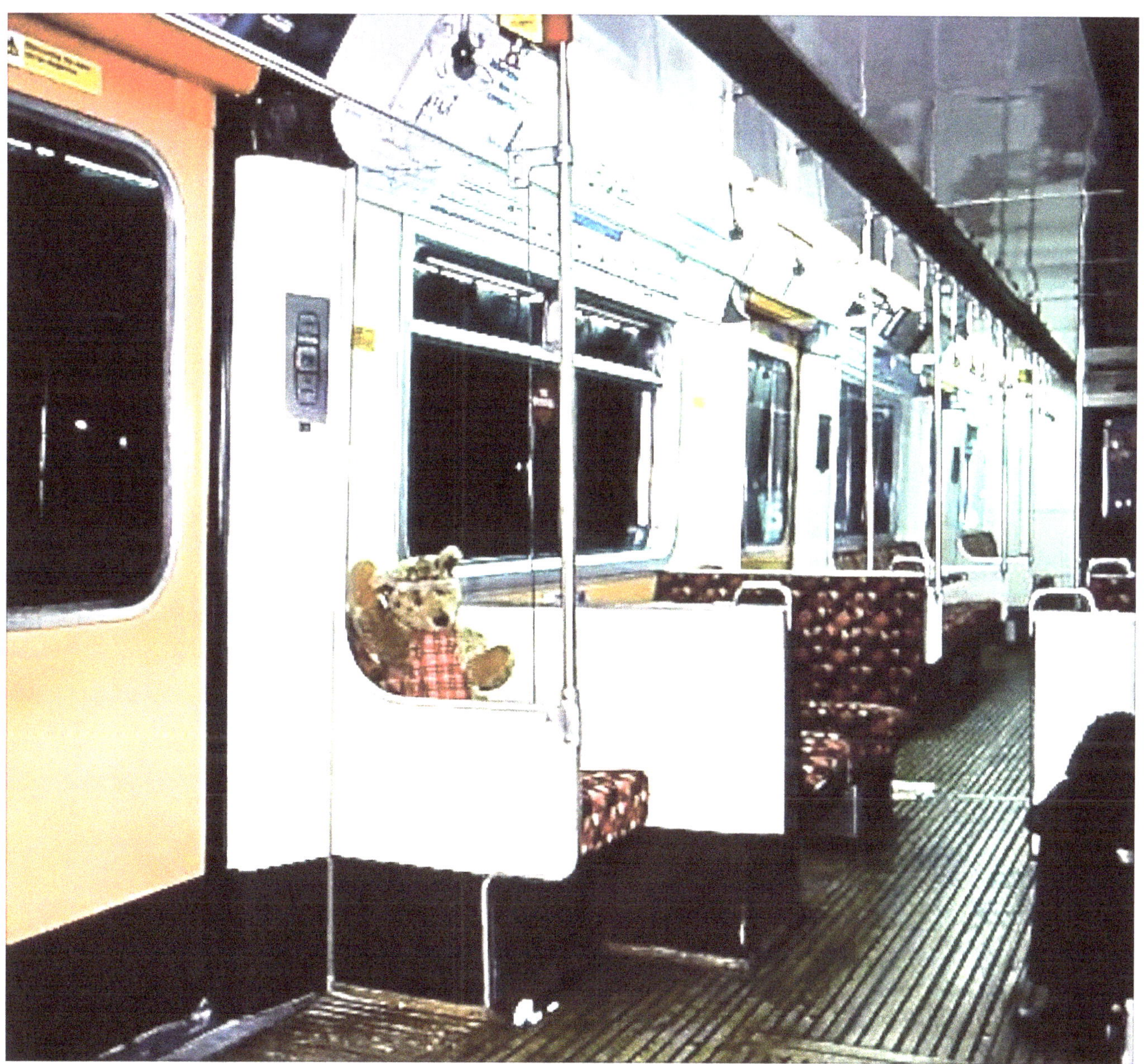

"Here we go, Dusty. We are off to find Uncle Willy and have an adventure."

"*Woof.* Are you sure you know how to drive this house? They wouldn't let you drive the big red bus."

"Bears can do anything."

"*Woof.* Dogs can't."

"That is why I am driving."

Information

A motorhome is a self-contained home combined with a vehicle. Beds are called berths and, depending on the size of the vehicle, can sleep up to 8 people. There is a small kitchen, bathroom and toilet and seating area. There is also a cab area for the driver and passenger.

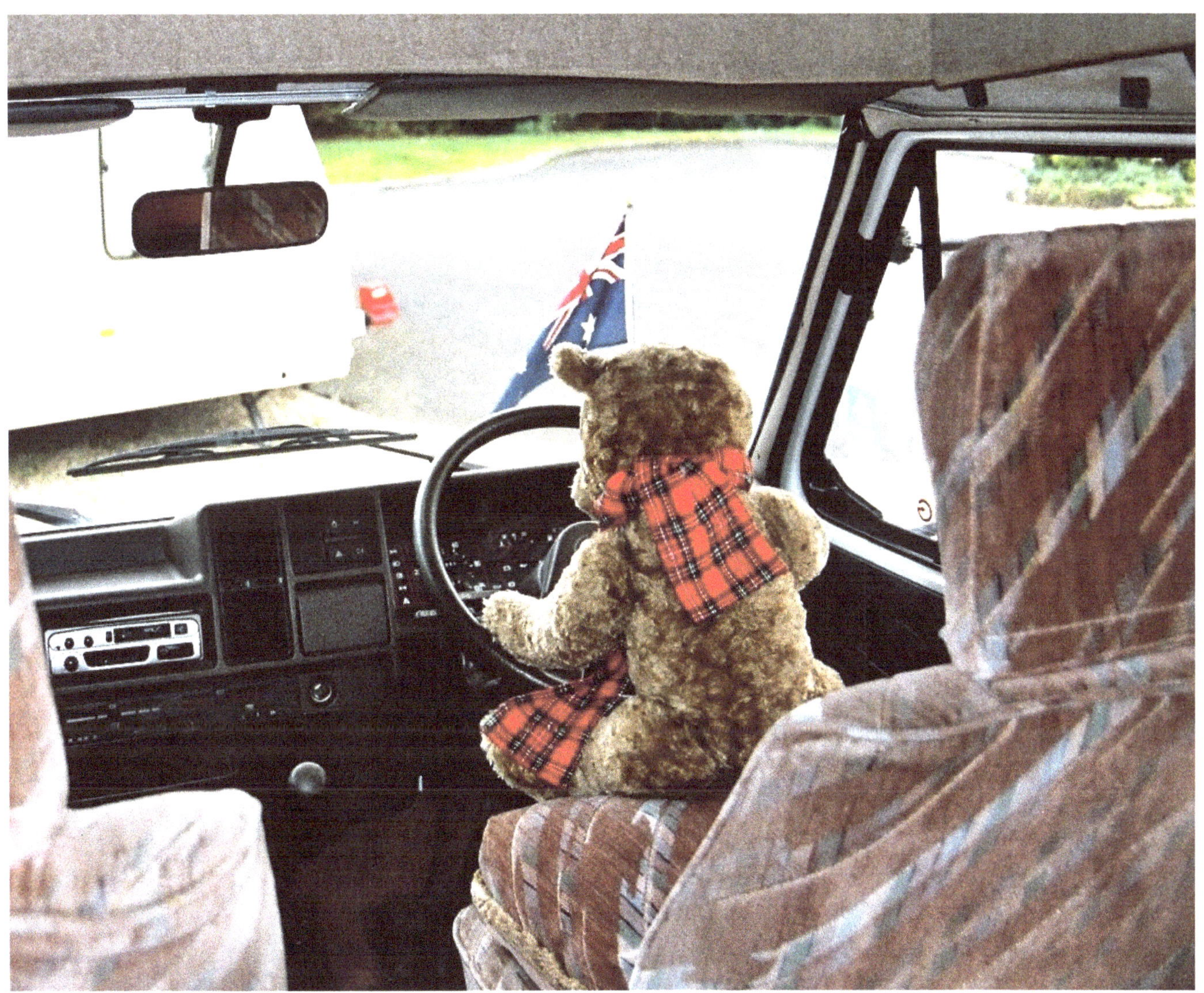

"Right, over the bridge we go and Ireland here we come. Dusty, you have the map upside down."

"*Woof.* B B, how do we get across to Ireland?"

"We drive onto a boat and the boat takes us across the sea."

"*WOOF.* A BOAT! You didn't tell me we were going on a boat. What if it sinks? I've only had two dog paddle lessons."

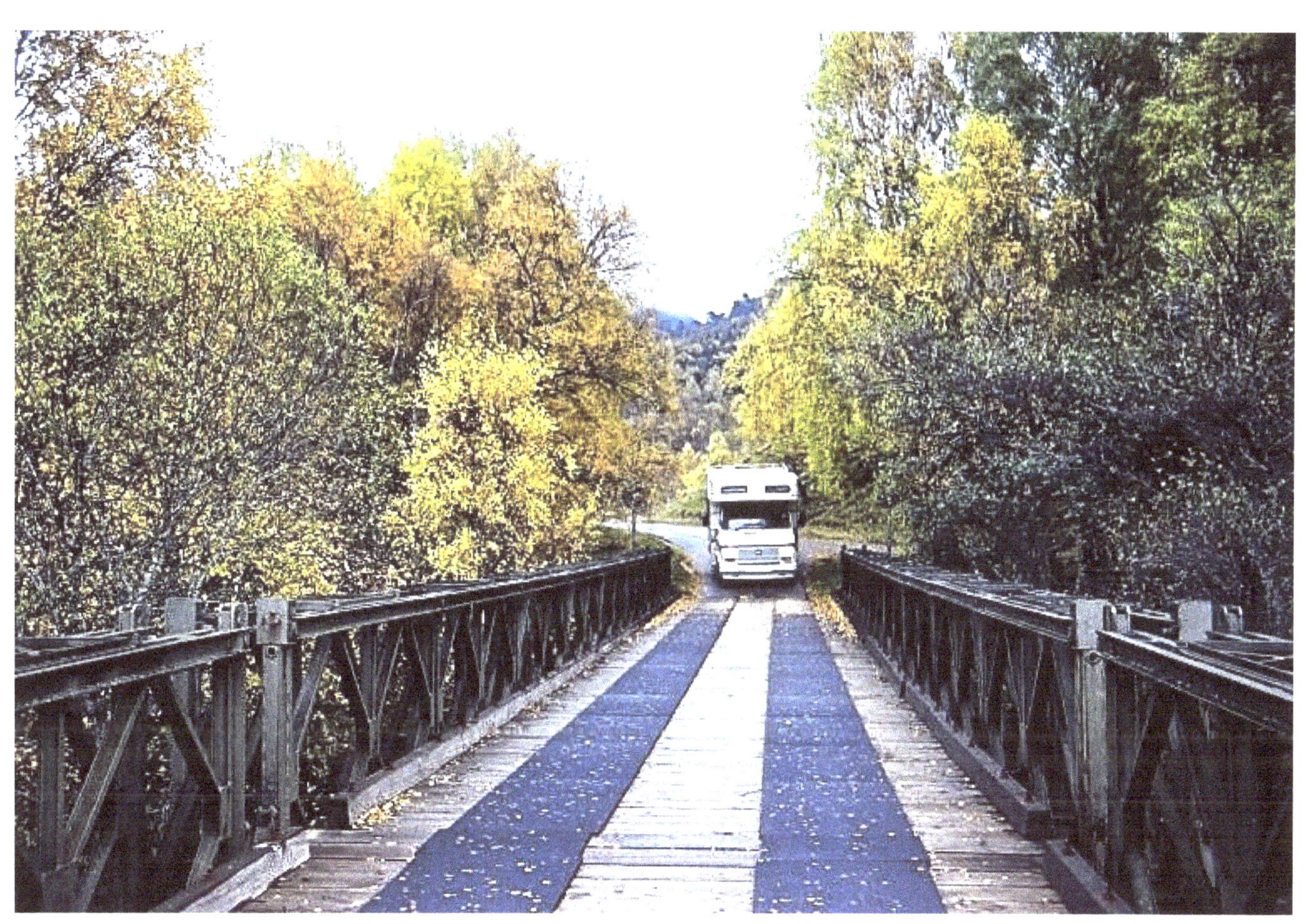

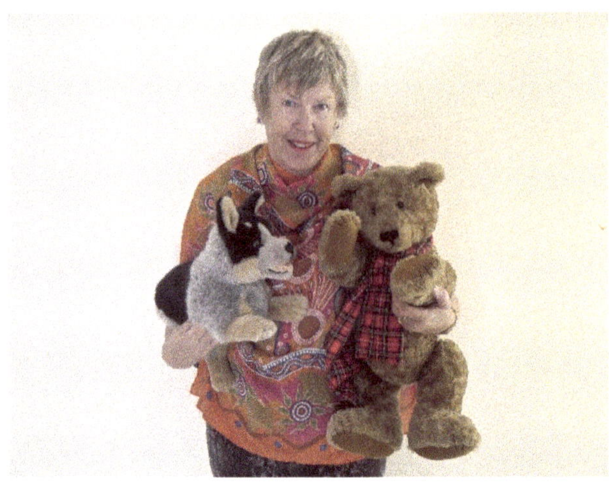

ABOUT THE AUTHOR

Born and educated in Perth, Western Australia, June is a keen traveller.

June wants adults and children to share her journey and learning experiences through the written word and photos. Using props of bear and dog, she and her husband Trevor spent twelve months touring England, Scotland, Wales and Ireland in a motorhome.

June is a trained photographer and has poems and short stories published in numerous anthologies. Her photographs and articles have been published in newspapers. Now retired, June, a member of The Society of Women Writers, Western Australia, is still viewing the world through the lens, and nib of her pen.

9 781876 922382